Arms of My Longing

Poems by
Kate Aver Avraham

BLUE LIGHT PRESS ◆ 1ST WORLD PUBLISHING

1st WORLD
PUBLISHING

SAN FRANCISCO ◆ FAIRFIELD ◆ DELHI

Winner of the 2020 Blue Light Poetry Prize

Arms of My Longing

BLUE LIGHT PRESS
www.bluelightpress.com
bluelightpress@aol.com

1ST WORLD PUBLISHING
PO Box 2211
Fairfield, IA 52556
www.1stworldpublishing.com

BOOK & COVER DESIGN
Melanie Gendron
melaniegendron999@gmail.com

COVER QUILT
Mary Kay Hamilton, Pacific Grove, Ca.
The quilt was adapted from a pattern designed by Carol McDowell.

AUTHOR PHOTO
Back cover photo: Rachel Katz
Inside photo: Lee Feathersong

FIRST EDITION

ISBN: 978-1-4218-3707-9

Praise for ARMS OF MY LONGING
Winner of the 2020 Blue Light Poetry Prize

It's long before light when I begin reading *Arms of My Longing*, which makes it kind of early to have anything to cry over, but tears begin because Avraham's poems remind me of what matters most, how the small, deeply experienced and witnessed moments add up to a life. I love that Avraham doesn't flinch; she turns toward the difficult. Though her loss is, of course, different from mine, these poems give me strength to bear my own sorrow and what I can of the world's, and they'll do that for you too. We all have those times "that hurt/ the way love does when it takes your lungs."

> – Patrice Vecchione, author of *My Shouting, Shattered, Whispering Voice: A Guide to Writing Poetry & Speaking Your Truth.*

The poems in *Arms of My Longing* tell an intimate and universal story of interconnection with the earth, ourselves and each other. The book explores motherhood, family, memory, and all that holds humanity together, and we are carried away by a great song from poem to poem. Nourishing, rich with verdant passages that one wants to read aloud and cherish, *Arms of My Longing* looks at the tragedies of life alongside its beauty and joy. I am enriched, my heart gladdened, having read it.

> – Carolyn Brigit Flynn, author of *Communion* and editor of *Sisters Singing* and *Sacred Stone, Sacred Water*

The title and the poems in Kate Avraham's *Arms of My Longing* extend backward to those the writer has lost – a son who died young, beloved father and mother – and forward to a daughter carving out her own life, and to the woman the writer is becoming, someone who can "ride along in just a red tank top even though/your arms are a little flabby." Arms and hands appear in many of the poems, and the urge for touch, for contact, or even simple recognition, runs like a thread through the fine weave of these elegiac, praise poems. At times the connotations are political-sociological: "Think of all those weathered hands/ plucking one plump strawberry at a time," and at other times exquisitely personal and pandemic-informed. The astonishing sequence about Nathan – who died at five – is moving precisely because the poems refuse to give into mourning and instead praise what the loss has brought home to the speaker. In "What the Meadow Gave," (which also suggests a meadow grave), she writes: "Nothing will ever bring you back.//And yet, this meadow grit/that presses against my skin//also mends." Reach out and let these poems touch you. Let them heal you. Our broken world needs them.

– David Sullivan, poet laureate of Santa Cruz County, Cabrillo College English professor and author of many books, including, *Strong-Armed Angels*; *Every Seed of the Pomegranate*; *Bombs Have Not Breakfasted Yet*; *Black Ice*. Coming out in 2021: *Black Butterflies Over Baghdad* and *Seed Shell Ash*.

For Jennifer, Laura and Melody

Contents

If you're already on the road at five a.m.

as the porcelain blue sky begins
to pale around its rim, and when you pass
the Langendorf bread truck, the man
waves to you like you're the only other
person awake in the whole world,
then down the road, you lift your cold can of
Mountain Dew to the driver of the Coca Cola van
and she laughs until the ash from her cigarette
drops off. You tune to AM, catch Carlos
Santana singing Black Magic Woman just as
you hit a stretch of road where you're all alone
so you speed up, straighten out those curves
the way your stock car-racing boyfriend taught you
thirty years ago. Then, if you're in the right place
when the edge of dawn yellows, you smell
the scent of dust in redwood trees as the sun
first reaches them. You downshift hard
instead of braking when you hit a curve
because it feels good, take off your shirt
ride along in just a red tank top even though
your arms are a little flabby, but you don't care
because the air has warmed up and you've rolled
all the windows down, so by the time the first flash
of sunlight hits your dash, turns it into shiny
silver chrome, your old Honda is rumbling
like a Harley and you know this is how to start over –
this is what it feels like to get a second chance.

If you slice an apple

lengthwise, you'll find cleavage
at the stem and crevices
where the dark seeds embed.
This will be true whether the apple
is red, gold or dappled.

You may also find a bruise
if the fruit was handled roughly
or perhaps a worm, eating avenues
into the core. Consider leaving the worm
alone, since he was there first.

Now, and you might remember this
from childhood, if you slice an apple
crosswise through its equator, you'll find
a five-pointed star, dropped there
from some other solar system –
every apple has one trapped inside.

Hold it in your hand, and
if you think of Eden remember
we have Eve to thank
for knowing evil would exist
no matter what, and for giving in
so we can all taste the sweetness.

Hands

Consider the hands
that pull plows across fields,
swing rakes and hoes,
till dark, expectant earth.

See the hands, palms turned upward,
lifelines deep and long,
cupping seeds that will slide
into damp awaiting soil.

Imagine the hands – brown, white, black –
gnarled, scarred from labor
hardly recognized,
fingers that grip broccoli, chard,
thorny artichoke so we can eat.

Think of all those weathered hands
plucking one plump strawberry at a time,
backs bent over one hundred eighty degrees,
sweat dripping like rain
onto the ground.

Taste the sweet red fruit,
let its juices burst forth in your mouth
as you remember the hands…

Laundry

When the surgeon finally called to say
benign, I couldn't take it in.
I'd been waiting five days, left breast
stitched like a train track.
His voice resembled a courtesy call:
Good news! No malignant cells in the lymph nodes…

No one home to tell, so I went
down the hall, threw a load of
wet laundry in the dryer,
wandered into the garage,
found a plastic funnel,
poured slick 10-30 into my Honda,
then wandered outside, yanked off
withered brown cosmos heads.

The wound began to throb.
I lay down on my bed, stared
at the lumpy stucco ceiling,
heard the doctor's words, over and over,
felt a brief moment that hurt
the way love does when it takes your lungs.
I drifted back to the laundry room,
pulled out the dry clothes…

…and suddenly the warm
soft flannel of old gray pajamas
became everything I had ever touched
every fiber alive
in the worn, miraculous fabric.

Cannas

What I remember most about the night
he held me down, took what I could no longer give,
are yellow cannas in a red vase on the table –
the way their petals splayed
to expose secret places,
how moonlight illuminated the thrust of stamen,
stigma covered in brown furry nectar.

The scene was perfect, except
for the absence of blue, primary blue
the absolute blue of ocean, sky
my father's honest eyes…
I wanted to reach into this still life with a brush
smear some azure here and there.

Frida Kahlo would have known
just how to do it.
Georgia O'Keefe would have ignored the red vase
completely, gone deep inside the flower
where it really mattered.

All I could do was lie in the linen hollow
my body had pressed into the bed,
notice chips and cracks in the red ceramic,
imagine myself rising up to lift
the yellow cannas from the water
wrap their stems and carry them out
into the livid darkness
of my parting.

Compassion

While listening to Nessi Gomes sing "All Related"

It's all so big…
from blue ocean emerging
out of morning fog,
to hearts that re-open
after searing grief
closed them for a long time.
Here, I am among fragrant white
jasmine flowers and fledgling crows.
A sea breeze caresses my skin
like a lover whose touch
you have waited all your life
to feel. And bliss
comes a thousand simple ways…
tray of cookies lifted
from a hot oven, or lyrics sung
that lead you home to yourself.
This morning I gave five dollars
to a kid on the street
who said he was hungry.
Everyone else ignored him
so when the money passed
between our hands
the gratitude in his eyes
filled me and compassion
became the thread that connects
everything.

Clinging

I am daily learning to be the reluctant guardian of your memories...
– Richard L. Ratliff

An avocado will not turn dark
as long as the flesh is connected to the pit.
Even if you cut it open, expose
the soft fruit to air or eat part of it,
what remains, nestled against its seed,
stays tender and green for a while.

I think of this as I watch you
cling to the core of yourself,
fight to remember where your shoes are,
the name of that man next door,
or how to sauté an onion in butter.
And sometimes, when too much is asked,
you wear that bruised expression,
as if the pit has been extracted and
you fear darkness will spoil everything.

Portal

Thick January night, I listen
to Yo-Yo Ma play Bach's cello suites,
all six of them, each note
wrested from the soul of genius.
Each tonal variation, a precipice
I climb up, then fall from.

Neither waking nor sleeping I ride
sound waves, preludes, sarabandes.
Time crescendos into brilliance,
defined by opacity, a pleasure
that aches like new love.

And just when C minor darkness gives way
to D major lightness of being...
I hear a cupboard door bang in the kitchen,
clink of a water glass extracted
as my father, lover of Bach,
gone twenty long years,
clears his throat, hums a few bass notes,
walks through the portal to join me.

Visitation, March 17

I'm at the stove adding
caraway seeds to corned beef
when she arrives, tells me
more onion, and never cook cabbage
in the same juice as potatoes.

I'm not surprised by her sudden appearance
or how she takes over,
ruddy face crinkled in delight,
white hair a wild halo.
She jabs the meat, stirs the broth,
calls me *Kathleen, mo mhuirnin, little darling,*
tells how she and Daddy chose my name
sitting close as cats under the willow tree
at Mesa Lane the very day
she found out she was pregnant.

Little splashes of juice shoot out like stars
as she flips the roast, whistles
"Irish Washerwoman," grabs my hands
for a jig across the scuffed wooden floor.
Long after the dance, I still hear her whistling,
go back to the bubbling pot,
add carrots, turn around to find
she has vanished again.

What Stayed with Me When I Drove Away

Two sunflowers, one upright
the other drooping,
stuck in a plastic water bottle
on the sill of her motel window.
My daughter, alone with her
Camel Lites and microwave pizza,
watched me pull away.
I could see her long, dark hair silhouetted
against the screen, strands grazing
the straps of a low-cut tank top
red as candied apples.

I had to stop looking.
So I wouldn't change my mind, go back
and climb the rotting stairs.
So I wouldn't pound on the scuffed door,
cross through clouds of smoke,
fold her into my arms
and take her home.

I pushed down on the accelerator,
gravel spewed from under the wheels.
In the rearview mirror, I chanced
a last glance – bright patch of yellow,
and her still standing at the window,
one small hand pressed
against the grimy mesh.

Devotion in Quarantine

My daughter's hands –
still small and slender
at age thirty-six,
fingers as graceful
as swaying meadow grass,
nails tapered to
crescent moon tips.

When she visits,
several times a week,
I hear her light step
on the deck stairs,
move chairs six feet apart
so we can safely sit together,
visit for a spell.

We raise our arms
over our heads in virtual hugs,
the way her older brother
used to do as the school bus
carried him off to kindergarten.

Then I watch those lovely hands
carry each full shopping bag,
set it gently on the outdoor table,
full of groceries to sustain us
while we shelter in place.

Remember

(for my granddaughter, Mia)

Remember the planet you were born under,
where it was in the sky
when you took your first breath.
There was never-ending brightness that day,
all because you were arriving.
Perhaps you came with arms outstretched,
ready to tackle this world again
or maybe it was your first time,
mouth and eyes wide open in amazement
as you slowly uncurled your limbs.

Stay amazed as long as you can.
It will help when, in spite of intentions,
your heart is shattered like a glass
falling from the highest shelf.

Most things can be mended on this earth.
It takes believing, which is why
I remind you to remember
the day you were born as a miracle,
you spinning with planets, sun, stars,
then growing in your mother's womb,
slipping out into the air,
your first cry startled, prophetic.

Night Before Women's March

Late night, sliver of moon –
wrapped in shadows I dream
I'm holding the limp bodies of children
who died at the southern border.
I swaddle them in linen,
lay them gently back into
their distraught parents' arms…

…startled, I awaken
damp with sweat and tears,
recognize this wall of grief
is the same one I couldn't climb over
after my own son died.

How can I say *I'm sorry?*
Apologize for a nation that has
torn itself apart with disregard
for the sanctity of all lives?

Only five a.m. I rise up from bed,
put my hiking boots, pink hat and
WHAT WOULD MLK DO? sign by the front door.
Later when I leave for the march, I know
I will carry the weight of those children
along the streets of my hometown.

Feeding, 2 a.m.

In remembrance of Nathan
May 16, 1979 to October 24, 1984

The middle of May. I wake suddenly
am surprised by the sight
of naked breasts sprawled across my chest,
loose flesh suffused in full moon's
blue-white, milky light.

The scene is eerie. Remorseful.
I notice my nipples are salmon pink
erect. They seem to remember
the seeking pucker of tiny lips, the voracious
tug of suckling that tingles, then flows
from ducts of love.

Oh, memory, stay with me
the way a mother does. Ample
and unending.

Pruning

For Nathan

The branch
on the old liquid amber
where you sat,
invincible king of everything
or hung from your knobby knees and
upside down asked why
baboons have orange behinds –

that branch is gone.
Cut off. By the gardener
who didn't know.

I wonder if the tree
feels a ghost limb
of pain, the way I do
when I look at the empty space
when I remember
the severing, when
like a tree with no limb

I miss you.

What the Meadow Gave

Quintet for Nathan

1.

I lie, belly down, in a dry autumn meadow
golden grasses cushion my flesh, my sweating
desire to remember.
I rest my cheek against mounding earth
the way a baby would splay across its mother's chest
when the nipple is empty.

I'm like this a long time, or maybe
it's only a moment that seems
like the prone forever we dream of.

2.

Though nothing I dream of
can bring you back
to lie beside me in this umber field.

Not a hundred dreams of raven
flying until she returns
from the blue-black canyon of death.

Not a thousand wishes blown
from the seed fluff of cottonweed
split open by copper slants of sun.

Not even the tawny coyote
mythic head bent skyward, howling
for one lost pup.

Nothing will ever bring you back.

3.

And yet, this meadow grit
that presses against my skin

also mends

this ground that stores the seasons
in its womb of dark dirt

warms me

and when I smell the musk
of earth's grasp on roots,
I can finally remember you beyond the dying,

4.

can finally see
your amber-brown eyes again,
how you rolled your fingers into fists
then flapped your thin arms
up and down in rhythm to a song,
perfect V at the nape of your neck
when you leaned over the table to color,

the cleft in your slightly jutting chin…

5.

…which I can hardly distinguish now from
a crevice in the granite cliff above me,

the amber eyes of autumn leaves
that blink when they flutter down,

your hands, fir branches, waving
in the deep, blue wind blowing

across the meadow

where I lie, belly down
holding the warm, dry ground

of you.

Perseids

Meteors fall
through midsummer night

white confetti
scattering silently

or with every sound
ever made.

This is how the universe
was born –

humble matter colliding
in all directions

askance, kinetic
as a Jackson Pollock painting

or like so much longing
it cannot be contained.

Later we learned
to breathe in, breathe out

give something back:
molecules of CO_2

or a kindness to someone
along the way.

Tonight, translucent slice
of new moon joins the stars…

Here is the beginning.

Here the perfect desire.

The Saying of Names

In this Sierra mountain canyon
I speak your name
to the gentle summer wind,
pronounce it slowly, with intent.
Each letter floats
over gurgling white water
of fresh snowmelt river.
Bright blue dragonflies ride
on the soft cursive designs of it,
wild white azaleas bless it
with the fragrance of their joy.
Ravens soaring high above
swoop to catch it in their beaks,
carry the sound of it far and wide
until it echoes its own desire.

A moment will come when you realize
I spoke your name in this way.
You will hear it return to you
on a warm summer breeze some afternoon...
and you will know it was me
who spoke it gently, with gladness.

Unrequited

Perhaps only the stars
will ever really know
what was pressed between
the pages of desire.

Hope of love, like wildflowers
collected after first dew,
or laughter, uncapped,
effervescent as a sparkling stream.

All along it was the someday
that no one could have –
shiny token still held fast
in your fist long after
the missed bus has pulled away.

And under all the words
given as freely as birds
finally let out of their cages...
there was unending light
that no one will see.

Multitude

(for the Ohlone People)

Here, we are
one tribe of beings
made of earth,
river, canyon, sandstone,
surging ocean.
We burst forth
like the bright orange
poppies that dot
our rolling green hillsides.
At night
we shimmer
with the same abundance
of stardust
that began us.

On our journey
we dance, sing, remember,
honor all lives –
two-legged upright;
four-footed with paws, claws;
feathered, flying;
cold-blooded, crawling;
swimmers in rivers
lakes, wetlands, sea;
earthbound growing things…
…the whole multitude
a kind of wild god
we always knew
but had almost forgotten.

Let There Be Grandmothers

My breath
fills this wooden flute,
echoes back to me
as if from inside
an old-growth tree.
I dwell in the tree.
The tree dwells in me.
We are birdsong
on the highest limb.
Both ancient, we call
to the ancestors,
ask them to walk
beside us as we march
for justice, protection
against pipelines, racism, war.
The hand drum joins in.
Low beat, heartbeat
of animal skin, wisdom.
Voice in the dark: *Let there be light!*
Let there be truth
and clean oceans,
forest and unpolluted air.

Let there be grandmothers
to tell stories
of past wars and grief.
They have washed
bodies of the dead,
know it's not enough
to just hope.

While there is still life
and a little wildness
left inside them, they say:
Go! Love, touch, dance,
chant together for peace –
fill flutes, drums,
the hearts of people
with songs of change.

Phoenix

In these hollow days of isolation,
I live in a wilderness
of redwood trees, raptors, tiny feeding birds,
peace as motionless
as a great-horned owl at midnight.

Chaos shudders everywhere else.
Contagion binds us all
to the reminder that nothing is forever.

Even Mother Earth shrugs
her resigned shoulders, tired
of begging us to intervene.

Outside my window, reluctant sun
plays coy with persistent gray gloom.
While I wait for emergent light,
the knife-sharp edge of grief
for every living thing cuts me.

Suddenly a red-shouldered hawk
lands on the fence outside,
swivels his commanding head until
his piercing gaze finds me…

I am drawn into a wisdom
far beyond my fragile aging self,
tired aching bones.

We have been scoured, scraped raw
to the core of what we've been
and may or may not become.

What we laid aside to make it through
falls short as paychecks, investments, dreams,
relationships collapse.
We are left looking at each other
naked and as real as when we were born.

Take up that infant of what is true,
cradle it close to your beating heart...
even Phoenix, burned to ashes,
rose again, renewed.

Just for a While Longer

I want to pry night open
until constellations pour stars
into the arms of my longing.
Want to ride on the light of another blue moon,
whip along with autumn wind
gusting in silver-lit trees.

I want to love, full on
in a tangle of limbs and lips,
then sigh for about an hour
because I feel like it.

Let me go into the streets,
greet people I don't know,
make eye contact with all those
windows into their souls.

I'm not done with this tender
merciless incarnation.

Just for a while longer
I want to feel life
jumping up inside me,
spinning me round and round
in circles of wonder.

THIS IS THE SWEATHOUSE USED FOR
CLEANSING AND RELIGIOUS PURPOSES
BECAUSE WE USE THIS HOUSE IN THE
OLD WAYS, WE ASK THAT YOU STAY
BEHIND THE BARRIER.
THANK YOU

About the Author

Kate Aver Avraham began writing and editing as a toddler, when she re-wrote all her picture books! She has been writing ever since: poetry, short fiction, memoir, and children's books.

Her chapter book, *Joey's Way*, was published in 1992 by MacMillan, Margaret McElderry books. In 2010, Kate's picture book, *What Will You Be, Sara Mee?* was published by Charlesbridge. The biography, *We Are All Related (The Life of Patrick Yana-hea Orozco in Recollections, Stories, Photos Songs and Dances)* appeared in 2019, Ravensong Press.

Kate's poetry has been published in many magazines, journals and anthologies, including *Calyx, A Journal of Art and Literature by Women; Nimrod International Journal; Porter Gulch Review; Sisters Singing*, edited by Carolyn Brigit Flynn; *Celebration of the Muse*, chapbook award winner for *Perhaps the Truth is Also Blue*; and most recently, *Mudfish 22*, Box Turtle Press.

In 1999, Kate founded Blue Moon Creations, a nonprofit endeavor benefiting charities and causes both locally and globally. In response to the pandemic, in 2020, Kate co-edited (with Melody Culver) the anthology *Second Wind: Words and Art of Hope and Resilience*, Fireball Press, with profits donated to the Covid-19 Relief Fund of the Community Foundation of Santa Cruz County. Future benefits projects include *Burgeoning*, an anthology of garden poems to benefit the Homeless Garden Project of Santa Cruz.

Kate is a native of Santa Cruz, where she grew up near the beach with her feet in the sand and the sea. You can find her at the shore every early March, diving into the chill Pacific for her birthday. She lives in Aptos at the edge of the redwood forest, where creatures great and small delight her and owls often sing her to sleep or suggest first lines for her next poems.

Acknowledgements

"If you're already on the road at five a.m." was published in *Mudfish 22*, Box Turtle Press

"Hands," "Clinging," and "Multitude" were published in the *Porter Gulch Review*

"What the Meadow Gave" was published in *Sister's Singing*, Ed. Carolyn Brigit Flynn

"Phoenix" was published in *Second Wind; Words and Art of Hope and Resilience*, Eds. Avraham and Culver

"Feeding 2 a.m.," "Cannas," and "If you slice an apple" were published in the *Nimrod International Journal*, and "If you slice an apple" was a finalist for the Pablo Neruda Prize

www.ingramcontent.com/pod-product-compliance
Lightning Source LLC
Chambersburg PA
CBHW021916040426
42447CB00007B/892